BALLANTINE BOOKS • NEW YORK

Published in the United States by Ballantine Books, a division of Random House, Inc., New York, and simultaneously in Canada by Random House of Canada Limited, Toronto.

Library of Congress Catalog Card Number: 90-93512

ISBN: 0-345-37226-3

Manufactured in the United States of America

First Edition: August 1991

10 9 8 7 6 5 4

YOU WANT THE TRUTH ABOUT CATS?...YOU'VE COME TO THE RIGHT PLACE
I'VE BEEN A CAT ALL OF MY LIVES, AND THE TRUTH **IS...**
TRUTH

CURIOSITY DOESN'T ALWAYS KILL THE CAT

SOMETIMES IT JUST MAKES HIM LOOK STUPID

A CAT WILL DO ANYTHING TO AVOID A VISIT TO THE VET

CATS WILL CHASE MICE

UNLESS THERE'S SOMETHING GOOD ON TV

A MEOWING CAT USUALLY WANTS SOMETHING

CATS CAN SEE IN THE DARK

JUST NOT VERY WELL

CATS ARE CREATURES OF HABIT

CATS CAN HEAR A CAN OPENER FROM A DISTANCE OF 12 MILES

CATS DON'T MAKE MISTAKES

THEY MAKE EXCUSES

WHAT HUMANS SEE
WHAT CATS SEE

CATS CAN RUN ABOUT 30 M.P.H.

60, IF GIRL SCOUT COOKIES ARE INVOLVED

CATS ARE SENSITIVE TO LOUD NOISES

CATS ARE LOYAL

UP TO A POINT

CATS HEAR

AND IGNORE

CATS ARE NATURAL CHARMERS

PROVIDED THEY HAVE THE RIGHT INSPIRATION

CATS KNOW BETTER

THEY JUST DON'T CARE

CATS AND CAR TRIPS

DON'T MIX

CATS HAVE A ROUGH TONGUE
FREEZE, SUCKER! ...DROP THAT DONUT!
AND THEY'RE NOT AFRAID TO USE IT

THE MORE YOU HATE TO VACUUM

THE MORE A CAT SHEDS

THE MOST COMFORTABLE SPOT FOR A CAT TO NAP

IS ANY SPOT YOU WERE ABOUT TO OCCUPY

ANY CAT CROSSING YOUR PATH IS BAD LUCK

CATS WASH THEMSELVES
WITH THEIR TONGUES

THE CLEANER THE CAT,
THE BIGGER THE HAIRBALLS

KNOW YOUR CAT MOODS
HAPPY
SAD
INWARDLY REMORSEFUL, YET CALMLY CONTEMPLATIVE
GURGLE
HUNGRY

WHAT HUMANS SEE
WHAT CATS SEE

CATS LOVE MILK

ESPECIALLY WHEN IT'S FRESH

CATS APPRECIATE BEAUTY IN ALL FORMS
♫
BURP
AND FLAVORS

CATS WILL USE SCRATCHING POSTS

BUT ONLY AS A LAST RESORT

A CAT'S COURAGE
IS EQUAL TO THE STRENGTH OF A DOG'S CHAIN

CATS NEED THEIR SPACE

AND YOUR SPACE, TOO

CATS JUST DON'T GIVE A HOOT

CATS HAVE RAISED SLEEPING TO AN ART FORM

CATS LOVE PLAYING WITH A BALL OF YARN

OR BETTER YET, A BALL OF PUPPIES

CATS DON'T ALWAYS LAND ON THEIR FEET

SOMETIMES THEY LAND ON THE DOG

A PURRING CAT
PURRRRRRRRRRRRRRRRRRRRRR
IS USUALLY CONTENT
A ROARING CAT
ROAAR
IS USUALLY A LION

YOU CAN TRAIN A CAT

BUT THEY'D RATHER TRAIN YOU

CATS KNOW HOW TO MAKE AN ENTRANCE

CATS ARE VERY PREDATORY

AND WILL STALK AND ATTACK AN ENTIRE HERD OF DONUTS

CATS RUSH IN WHERE SENSIBLE PETS NEVER GO

CATS ARE NOT BONELESS

IT ONLY SEEMS THAT WAY

CATS AREN'T FINICKY

AND PIGS HAVE WINGS

CATS WILL READILY DEFEND THEMSELVES

CATS AGE GRACEFULLY

MOST CATS DON'T OWN TEDDY BEARS

THOSE THAT DO, HOWEVER, ARE MUCH MORE WELL ADJUSTED

YOU NEVER KNOW WHAT THE CAT WILL DRAG IN

WHAT HUMANS SEE
WHAT CATS SEE

CATS DON'T DO GUILT

ADULT CATS REQUIRE ONLY ONE MEAL PER DAY

CATS IN LOVE

SOUND LIKE YAKS IN DISTRESS

A CAT RUBBING AGAINST YOUR LEG IS A SIGN OF AFFECTION

SOMETIMES

CATS CONSTANTLY CRAVE ATTENTION
HEY! OVER HERE!
WHOP!
SPOOT!

CATS HISS WHEN THEY ARE ANGRY

OR WHEN THEY HAVE A SLOW LEAK

CATS ARE NOT LAZY
Z

CATS HATE BEING RUBBED THE WRONG WAY

CATS ALWAYS HAVE TO HAVE THE LAST LAUGH

CATS ARE BIG ON GIVING

CATS HAVE THEIR HEROES

CATS DON'T HOLD GRUDGES

THEY GET EVEN RIGHT AWAY

WHAT HUMANS SEE
WHAT CATS SEE
SALAD BAR

A CAT'S FACE MAY SAY ONE THING

BUT THE TRUTH IS IN THE TAIL

CATS HAVE 9 LIVES

BECAUSE THEY NEED ALL THEY CAN GET

IN OTHER WORDS, CATS ARE NATURE'S WAY OF PROVING THAT PERFECTION IS POSSIBLE...

AND THAT'S THE TRUTH

... TRUST ME